TAYLOR SWIFT OUTFITS COLORING BOOK

BOLD AND EASY DESIGNS FOR SWIFTIES

THIS COLORING BOOK BELONGS TO THE ULTIMATE SWIFTIE

____

Published by
GRAPEVINE BOOKS

www.grapevinebooks.com
Delhi | Mumbai
email: grapevineindiapublishers@gmail.com

Ordering Information:
Quantity sales: Special discounts are available on quantity purchases by corporations, associations, and others.
For details, reach out to the publisher.

First published by Grapevine Books 2025

NOT A LOT
GOING ON
AT THE
MOMENT

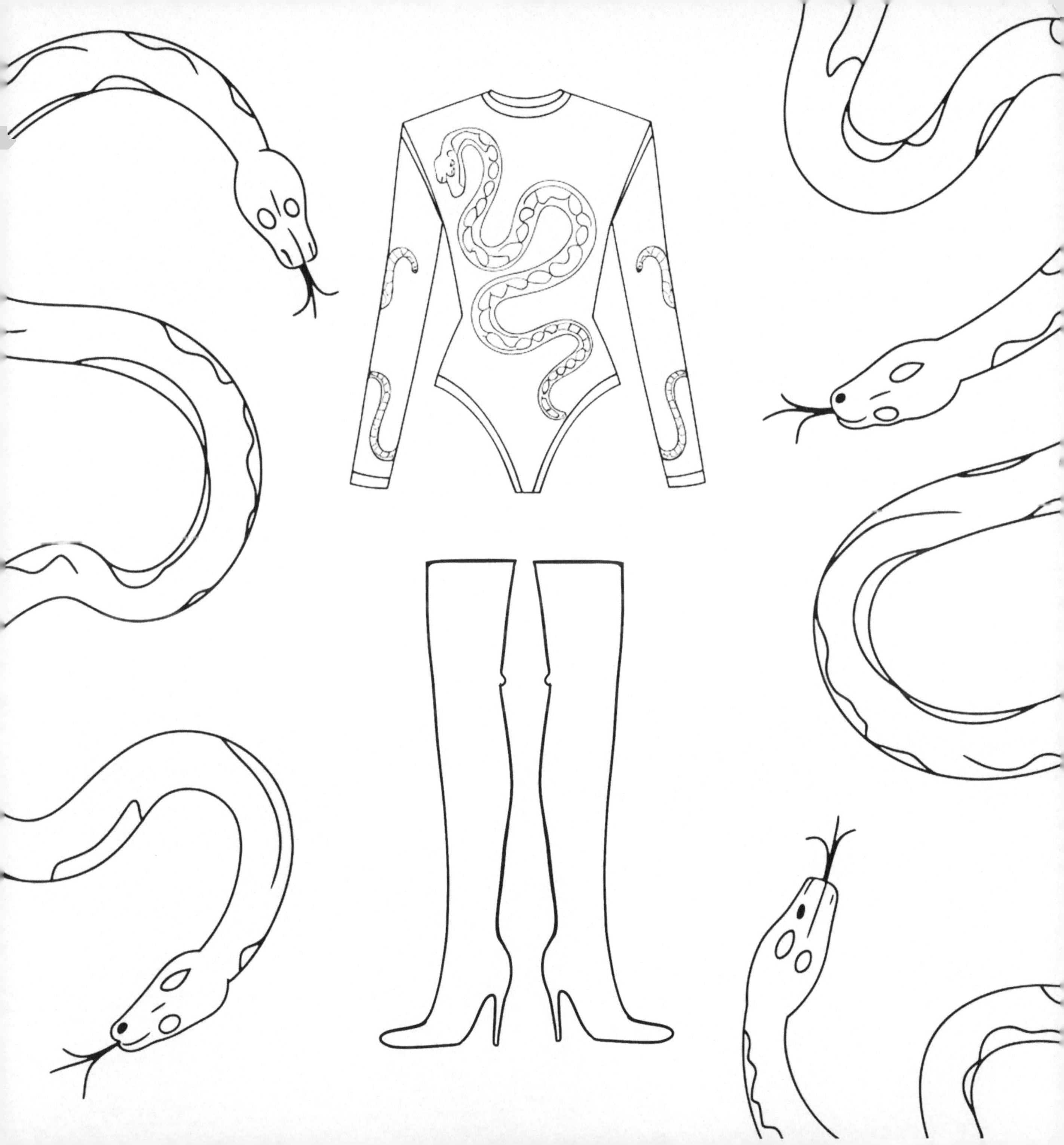

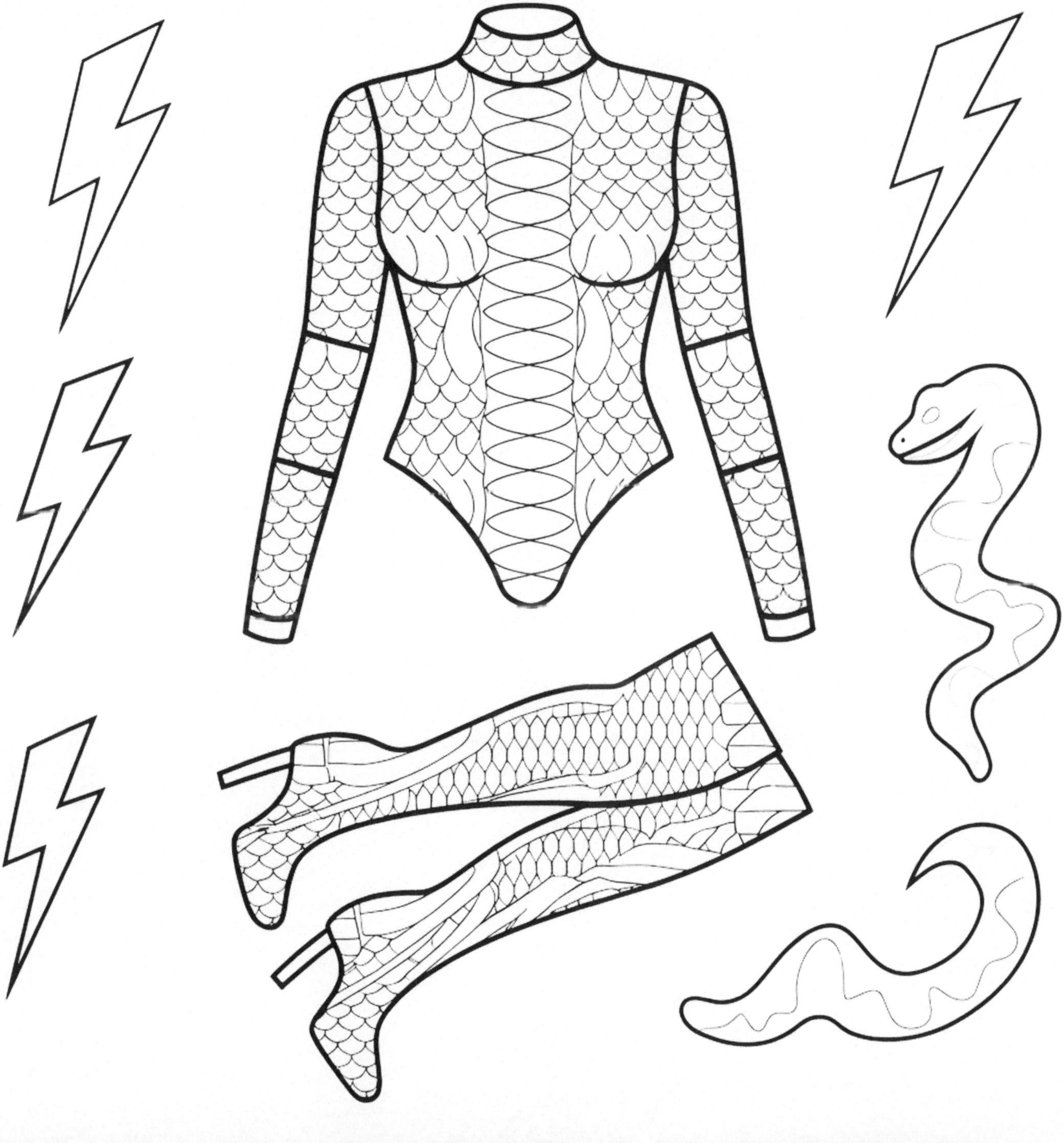

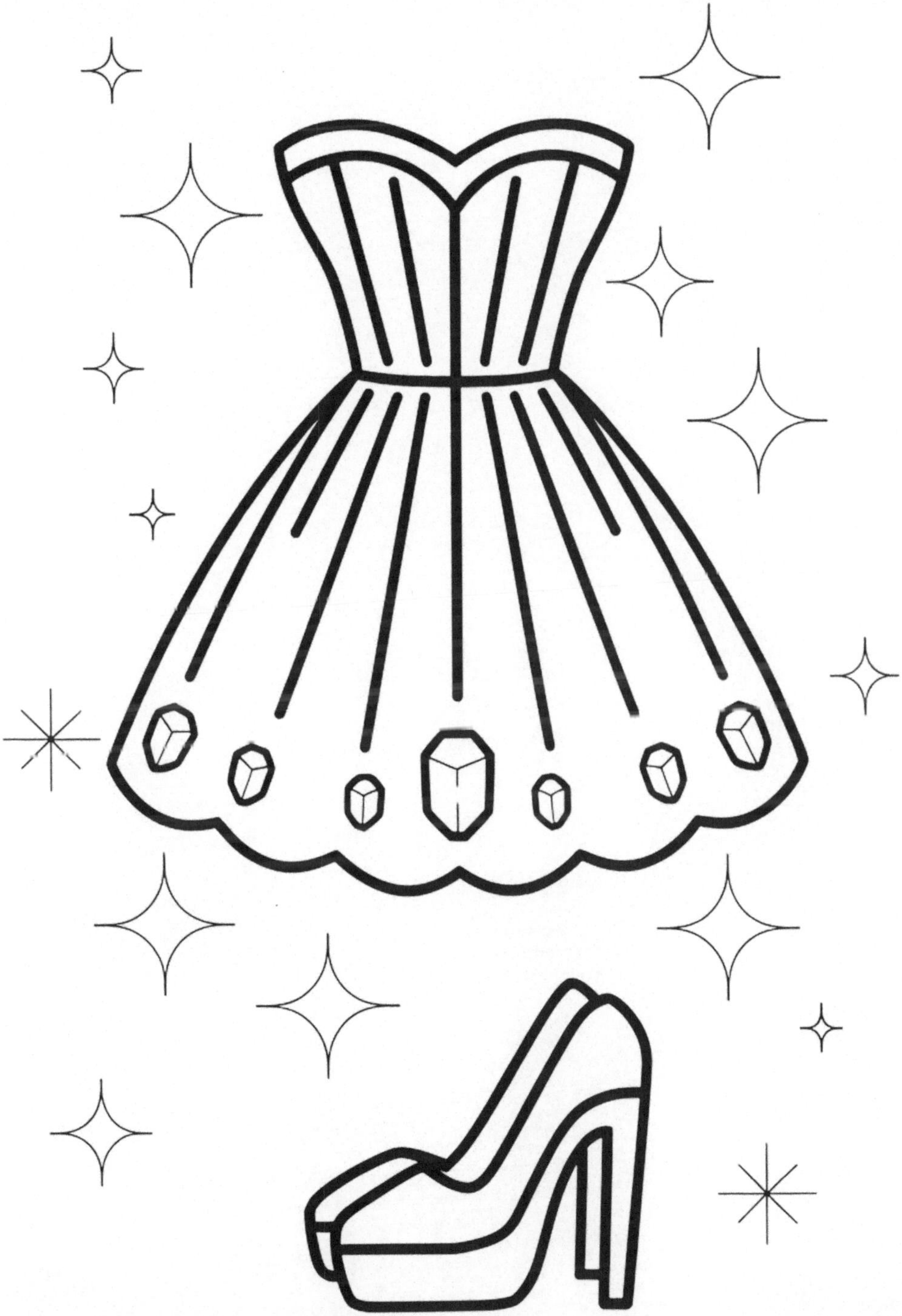

Taylor
Swift

TAYLOR
SWIFT

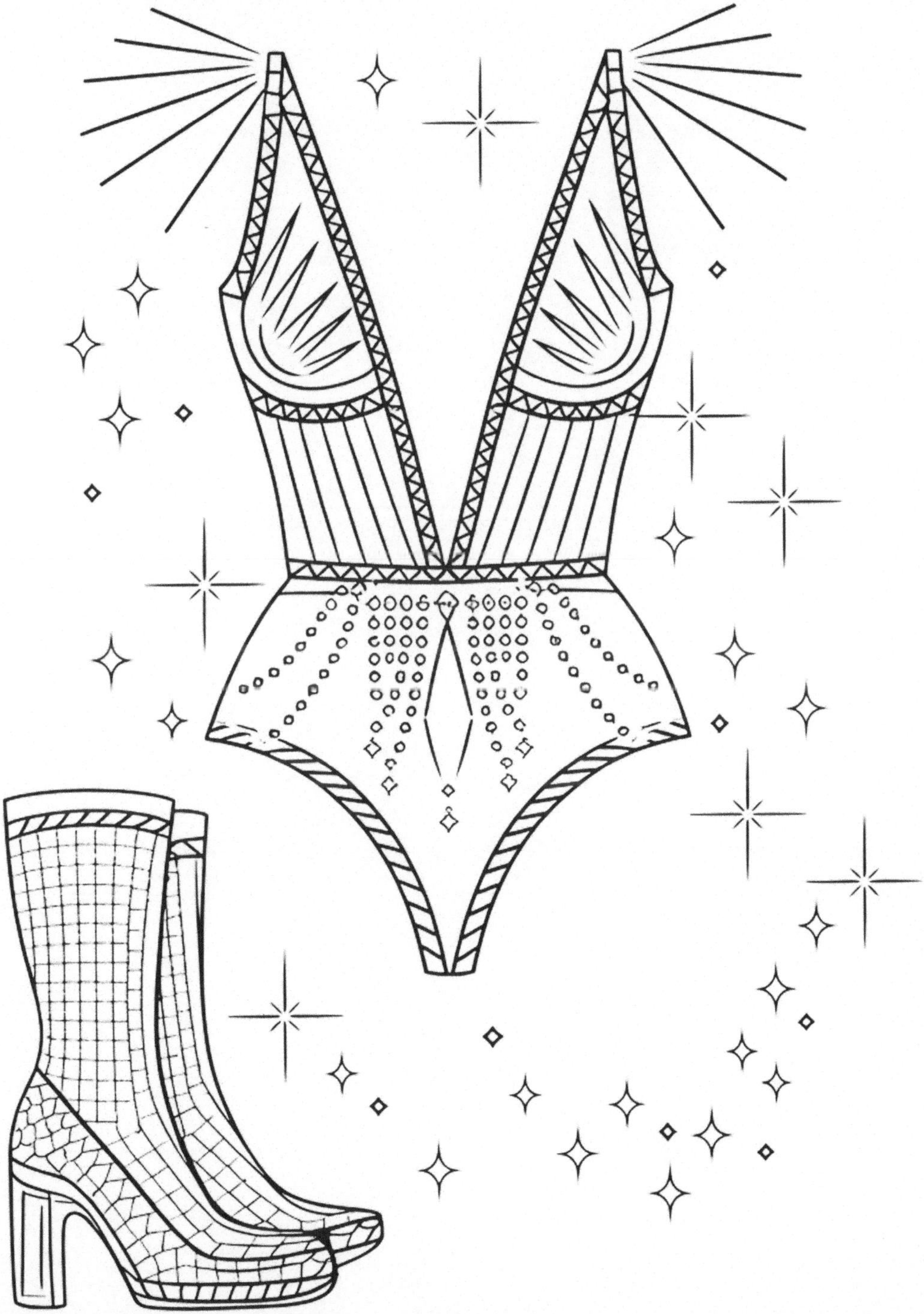